Dear Deer

inspired by true story

by Mary Kay Worth

illustrated by Mark Del Villar

Ordering Information:
You may search this book in Amazon, Barnes & Nobles and other online retailers by searching using the ISBN below.

ISBN (eBook):   978-1-958920-08-4
ISBN (Paperback):   978-1-958920-07-7
ISBN (Hardback):   978-1-958920-06-0

DEDICATION

You. I was led to you in King Ferry. The blue truck was there.
You. I browsed the old farmhouse second floor and coveted and bought.
You. I took every visitor I could to Ferry Tales.
You. I shared your passion for special education and quirky art.
You. I listened and kept the altered book, LIVE, you made.
You. Brought the store to me when I could no longer navigate the stairs.
You. I listened and kept the altered book, LISTEN TO YOUR ANGEL, you made.
You. I call you my friend.

This is for you, Chris Wilbur. You are special.
You are loved. You know Lucky Stones.

You are wild. A seven-point rack.
You should run. But you didn't.
You came close. One day following my dog,
following me along Lake Road.
Another time you trailed behind a Great Dane.
I got close. Within six feet.
Why weren't you afraid? Why didn't you run?

1

Near sunset. Walking my dog. Not far to the park.
Families gathered, enjoying the new playground.
A last late summer day before school began.

You were there, too. In the middle.
Adults and children approached. Within six feet.
Why weren't you afraid? Why didn't you run?

3

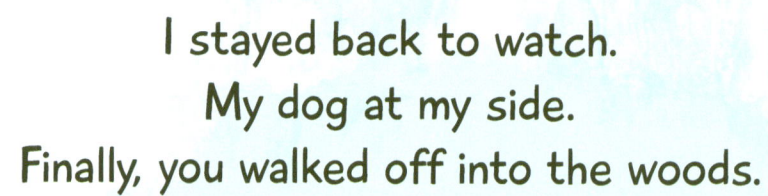

I stayed back to watch.
My dog at my side.
Finally, you walked off into the woods.

Chatter. Stories spinning.
"Did you see the deer? Did you get close?"
Dear Deer, why weren't you afraid?
Why didn't you run?

Through the tiny park.
Around the Point.
Boat launch. Now the stairs.
Up. Up. Up.

A parking lot. Not empty.
Tall and proud. Dear Deer.
You were there.
Why weren't you afraid?
Why didn't you run?

7

The dog at my side.
Leash held tight.
A buck. The rack.
Full in velvet. A yearling.
Faint spots still visible
along your spine.

Our eyes locked. You stepped.
I stayed. Closer. Closer you came.
Three feet.
Why weren't you afraid?
Why didn't you run?

9

And then, Dear Deer, you took one more step.
Too close for the dog. Both startled.
It was time to head home.

Certainly, it was over.
But no. You followed.
Why weren't you afraid? Why didn't you run?

The dog. Me. You.
Walking down Lake Road.
Together.

Neighbors were called. Witnesses needed.
One touched along your spots.
Why weren't you afraid? Why didn't you run?

13

Up the dirt road. 75 yards.
Three walked. Together.

At the house, the dog put in.
Now just two. Face to face.
Eye to eye. Why weren't you afraid?
Why didn't you run?

15

Dear Deer came closer.
I reached out.
I touched your face.
I brushed antler velvet.

16

No fear.
Why weren't you afraid?
Why didn't you run?

17

Now inside. It was over.
No dream. Only wonder.
Never seeing you again, Dear Deer.

Hunting season was coming.
I wanted you to be afraid.
Why weren't you afraid? Why didn't you run?

19

Child of God, Grandma, Mother, Daughter, Sister, Friend
Person with Disabilities
Teacher, Principal, Superintendent, Professor
Traveler, Storyteller, Photographer, Actor,
Musician, Author, Owner

Mary Kay is a native of Portville, NY, and now lives in Hampton, VA. Following 30+ years in public education, Mary Kay has nine titles: *HEY ELEPHANT! WHERE ARE YOU?* , *Banele – the Girl from Swaziland*, *Mountains Trees Plant and Flowers of Swaziland*, *Dear Deer*, *The Truth About Santa*, *Three Christmas Stories*, *Pop Pop's Train Ride*, *The Great Train Robbery*, and *A Lucky Stone Day*.

Good River Print and Media has illustrated best sellers and book #9.

Available through Mary Kay's website or Amazon.

For more information check out Mary Kay's website:

www.marykayworthofficial.com